SHADOWS OF VALOR

NAVIGATING IMPOSTER SYNDROME WHILE SERVING IN THE U.S. MILITARY

DR. JOSHAN A. FLOWERS, DSL

ISBN: 978-1-964898-19-3 (paperback)
978-1-964898-13-1 (hardcover)

Published by:
Pine Book Writing
www.PineBookWriting.com
R-10225 Yonge St Suite #250, Richmond Hill, ON L4C 3B2, Canada.

Printed in the United States of America

DEDICATION

To all the men and women serving in the U.S. military who may be grappling with mental health challenges, just as I did throughout my career. Your strength and resilience are an inspiration. And to those who are not, I urge you to offer unwavering support to your fellow service members who are facing these battles. Together, we can foster an environment of understanding, compassion, and hope.

ACKNOWLEDGMENT

I would like to extend my deepest gratitude to my husband, Ramni, whose unwavering support and love have been my cornerstone. To my son, Billah, and my daughter, Hadiyyah, your boundless encouragement and belief in me have been a constant source of inspiration.

I also wish to acknowledge all the incredible men and women I had the honor of serving with throughout my military career. From my beginnings with Honor Flight W/068 to my tenure with those on the Joint Chiefs of Staff, each of you has left an indelible mark on my journey. Your camaraderie, dedication, and shared experiences have profoundly shaped who I am today.

Thank you all for being part of this remarkable journey.

PROLOGUE

On the first day of Air Force Basic Training, at Lackland Air Force Base, I found myself as a 20-year-old from Chicago among 40 women who had just arrived for training. After we collected our luggage and headed to the Bay Area, which would be our home for the next six weeks, the Training Instructor (TI) gathered us and determined the leadership positions for our flight. To my astonishment, I was selected as an Element Leader, one of five positions responsible for guiding and directing other women in the flight. This came as a shock to me as I had never been particularly outgoing or held a leadership role before. I questioned why I was chosen, convinced it was a mistake, and anticipated that the TI would soon correct it by picking someone else. If I had known what Imposter Syndrome was then I would have understood what those feelings of self-doubt I was experiencing were. However, I managed to fulfill my duties as Element Leader for the entire six weeks, and our flight was honored with the title of Honor Flight, due to my contributions as a leader.

Imposter syndrome is a psychological phenomenon characterized by individuals experiencing doubt regarding their own accomplishments and harboring a constant fear of being revealed as a "fraud," even in the presence of evidence demonstrating their competence. Those who encounter imposter syndrome frequently attribute their success to luck or external factors rather than recognizing their own capabilities, resulting in feelings of inadequacy, anxiety, and self-doubt. This pattern is commonly observed among high achievers and can significantly affect various areas of life, including work, relationships, and personal growth.

Imposter syndrome can profoundly affect individuals, especially in the structured military environment. It often leads to feelings of inadequacy, self-doubt, and fear of being discovered as a fraud, even when there is evidence of competence. In the military, where proficiency, leadership, and teamwork are highly valued, imposter syndrome can worsen these feelings due to the high expectations placed on service members. Within the military community, imposter syndrome can have a significant impact. Service members may feel pressured to meet standards of bravery, competence, and resilience, causing them to internalize their doubts and fears. As a result, there can be a culture of silence around mental health issues, as individuals fear being perceived as weak or unfit if they admit to struggling with imposter syndrome or other psychological challenges.

The struggles faced by service members experiencing imposter syndrome are complex. Despite evidence of success and recognition, they consistently doubt their abilities and qualifications. This constant self-doubt can lead to chronic stress, anxiety, and burnout as they try to prove their worth. Imposter syndrome also affects decision-making and confidence in leadership positions. Service members experiencing imposter syndrome may hesitate to assert themselves or take risks for fear of failure or being exposed. This can undermine unit cohesion and effectiveness, especially in high-pressure situations.

Imposter syndrome, a term coined by psychologists Pauline Clance and Suzanne Imes in 1978, refers to a psychological pattern where individuals doubt their accomplishments and fear being exposed as frauds, even though they are competent. This concept gained traction across various fields, including the military, as it became evident that even high-achieving individuals could struggle with feelings of inadequacy and self-doubt. In the military context, impostor syndrome has historical roots in the demanding nature of military service. Those serving are frequently thrust into high-pressure situations and are expected to perform at their best consistently. Airmen, Soldiers, Marines, Sailors, and Coast Guardsmen can grapple with doubts about their abilities, feeling as though they don't truly deserve their positions or achievements. Over time, there has been a growing recognition of the psychological challenges faced by military personnel, including impostor syndrome. The hope for the military is with a better understanding of this mental health issue, efforts to address impostor syndrome within the military will expand. These initiatives could include leadership training, mentorship programs, and support networks that aim to foster resilience and self-confidence among service members.

In the current military environment, dealing with impostor syndrome is particularly important due to the complex and rapidly changing nature of modern warfare. Military personnel must adapt to new technologies, navigate diverse cultural landscapes, and operate in volatile, uncertain, complex, and ambiguous (VUCA) environments. In such settings, self-assurance and confidence in one's abilities are crucial for effective decision-making and leadership. Furthermore, if impostor syndrome is not addressed, it can have negative effects on both individual well-being and organizational performance. It may contribute to stress, burnout, and decreased performance among military personnel, ultimately undermining unit cohesion and mission success.

Recognizing and addressing impostor syndrome in the military requires a multi-faceted approach that involves promoting psychological resilience, providing mentorship and support networks, and fostering a culture that values honesty, vulnerability, and self-reflection. By empowering service members to recognize and overcome feelings of inadequacy, the military can cultivate a more confident and resilient force capable of meeting the challenges of the 21st-century security landscape. "Shadows of Valor" highlights the resilience and strength of veterans facing impostor syndrome. The central theme focuses on the path to self-acceptance and overcoming internal obstacles that hinder growth. Through shared experiences and valuable lessons, the book serves to inspire readers, both within and outside the military community, to acknowledge their own worth, embrace their achievements, and navigate impostor syndrome with bravery and authenticity.

Embark on a journey of exploration, learning, and personal growth through the pages of this book as we delve into the intricate landscape of impostor syndrome. Whether you are a seasoned veteran, a fresh recruit, or somewhere in between, this journey offers invaluable insights and tools to navigate the challenges of self-doubt and insecurity.

As you flip through the pages, I encourage you to think about your own experiences and perspectives on imposter syndrome. Can you recall moments in your life when doubt overshadowed your achievements? When have you felt like you didn't belong, despite your accomplishments? By exploring these questions, you'll gain a deeper understanding of the underlying dynamics of imposter syndrome and how it affects your life and career. This journey isn't just about self-reflection, though—it's also about empowerment. Through stories of resilience, strategies for self-compassion, and practical exercises, you'll discover how to confront imposter syndrome directly and cultivate confidence and authenticity. You'll learn to recognize the voice of the imposter within and reclaim your sense of worthiness in the face of self-doubt.

I invite you to embark on this transformative journey with me. Together, let us navigate the twists and turns of imposter syndrome, emerging on the other side as stronger, more resilient, and more self-assured individuals. Though the path ahead may be challenging, the rewards of self-discovery and personal growth await those who dare to embark on it.

TABLE OF CONTENTS

CHAPTER 1

THE SILENT STRUGGLE
INTRODUCTION TO IMPOSTER SYNDROME

Imposter syndrome is a psychological phenomenon characterized by persistent feelings of self-doubt and inadequacy, despite evident accomplishments. It can have a unique manifestation within the military, potentially affecting both operational effectiveness and individual well-being. This chapter aims to delve into the definition of imposter syndrome, explore its prevalence within military ranks, and analyze its impact on service members.

Imposter syndrome is a psychological condition characterized by a lack of confidence and a persistent feeling of incompetence, irrespective of one's accomplishments. It prevents individuals from experiencing the satisfaction of success as they continually anticipate being exposed as inadequate and fraudulent.

The imposter phenomenon stems from a sense of inadequacy within one's environment, despite objective evidence of competence. What distinguishes it is that it is not related to the evaluation of external circumstances, but rather the evaluation of oneself. Those with imposter syndrome often perceive themselves as more inadequate than others when confronted with similar complex situations, to the extent that they question their own belongingness.

Imposter syndrome can generate a sense of urgency and anxiety, as if time is running out. It feels as though individuals have been maintaining a façade and can no longer sustain it, despite all evidence suggesting otherwise. It is crucial to recognize that these thoughts and feelings persist even after individuals have achieved and overcome numerous challenges in their lives.

Many high achievers eventually reach a stage in their careers where they begin to doubt their ability to sustain their performance. This can lead to feelings of shame. This sense of shame often compels individuals to suffer in silence, as they fear confessing their struggles to others. Consequently, the prevalence of imposter syndrome remains largely unknown.

After successfully completing Air Force Basic Training, I proceeded to Technical Training School at Brooks Air Force Base. The atmosphere there mirrored that of Basic Training, albeit with greater freedom of movement. While the instructors displayed a somewhat less rigid demeanor than during Basic Training, they upheld their authority and rank. Once again, I was selected for a leadership role, this time as a Green Rope for my Flight. As a Green Rope, my responsibilities encompassed overseeing all Airmen within my flight and guiding them to and from classes.

Despite having previously served as an Element Leader during basic training, I did not anticipate being chosen once again. I anxiously waited for the moment when the instructor might reconsider their decision and utter, "I apologize, I made an error." However, that moment never transpired. Contending with Imposter Syndrome remained a persistent challenge for me, often leading me to question my suitability for advancements or recognition. Nevertheless, the truth was that I truly merited the distinction and performed exceptionally well as a leader.

In the military context, imposter syndrome can arise due to the stringent standards upheld within the organization. Service members are continuously evaluated, promoted, and entrusted with responsibilities that carry significant weight. Despite meeting or exceeding these standards, some individuals may perceive themselves as unworthy or unqualified, fostering a sense of fraudulence.

The prevalence of imposter syndrome within military ranks is influenced by various factors, including organizational culture, individual experiences, and societal expectations. While empirical data specific to the military is limited, anecdotal evidence and psychological research suggest that imposter syndrome is prevalent among service members across different branches and ranks.

One contributing factor to the prevalence of imposter syndrome in the military is the culture of perfectionism and high expectations. Service members are trained to strive for excellence, often facing intense scrutiny and pressure to perform flawlessly in their duties. This constant pursuit of perfection can exacerbate feelings of inadequacy, especially when combined with the inherent stressors of military life, such as combat deployments and demanding training exercises.

Moreover, the hierarchical structure of the military can amplify imposter syndrome among junior enlisted personnel and junior officers. Individuals at lower ranks may compare themselves unfavorably to their superiors, feeling as though they do not measure up to the standards set by those in positions of authority.

Additionally, the competitive nature of career progression within the military can fuel imposter syndrome, as service members vie for promotions and recognition. The impact of imposter syndrome on service members is far-reaching and detrimental. It hinders their ability to perform at their full potential and contribute effectively to their teams. Moreover, it results in heightened stress, lower self-esteem, and a perpetual cycle of self-doubt. Addressing imposter syndrome within the military is crucial for enhancing overall well-being and optimizing operational effectiveness.

Imposter syndrome can have a profound impact on service members, affecting their well-being, operational effectiveness, and unit cohesiveness. Those grappling with imposter syndrome can experience heightened stress, diminished confidence, and impaired performance.

One significant consequence is increased stress and anxiety levels. Service members who constantly feel inadequate fear being exposed as frauds, leading to chronic stress and anxiety about their abilities. This stress can harm mental and physical health, potentially causing burnout, depression, and other psychological disorders.

Imposter syndrome can also erode self-confidence and self-esteem, undermining a service member's sense of identity and purpose. Despite their accomplishments and qualifications, those struggling with imposter syndrome may doubt themselves and downplay their achievements, perpetuating a cycle of negativity.

In terms of operational effectiveness, imposter syndrome can hinder performance and decision-making, especially in high-stakes situations. Service members preoccupied with feelings of inadequacy may hesitate or second-guess their decisions, potentially compromising mission success. Furthermore, imposter syndrome can strain interpersonal relationships and diminish unit unanimity. Service members who feel like imposters may struggle to trust their peers or seek support, fearing judgment or ridicule. This lack of trust and communication can undermine teamwork and camaraderie, hindering effectiveness and morale. Imposter syndrome presents a significant psychological challenge in the military, affecting service members of all ranks and branches. It is characterized by persistent uncertainty and feelings of imperfection, with consequences that extend to individual well-being, operational effectiveness, and unit rapport.

Addressing imposter syndrome requires a comprehensive approach that includes both individual and organizational interventions. It is crucial to provide service members with education and support to recognize and manage imposter syndrome, fostering resilience and self-assurance. Additionally, fostering a climate of psychological safety and mutual support within military units can effectively reduce the stigma around seeking assistance for mental health concerns, including imposter syndrome.

By recognizing the prevalence and impact of imposter syndrome in the military and implementing targeted measures to combat it, military leaders can empower service members to overcome self-doubt and thrive in their duties, greatly enhancing their preparedness and ability to successfully accomplish missions.

CHAPTER 2

THE FOUNDATION OF VALOR
UNDERSTANDING MILITARY IDENTITY

Exploring Unique Identity Challenges Faced by Service Members

Service members in the United States Military face a variety of unique identity challenges due to the distinct nature of military life. The rigorous demands of military service, including adherence to strict protocols, maintaining peak physical condition, and developing specialized skills, create an environment that profoundly shapes one's identity. These demands often lead to a dual existence where service members balance their military identity with their personal lives.

The highly structured environment of the United States Military, with its emphasis on discipline, hierarchy, and a collective mission, can instill a strong sense of belonging and pride. However, it can also lead to feelings of isolation from those outside the military who may not fully understand the experience. The transient nature of military assignments and deployments adds another layer of complexity, as constant relocations and the possibility of combat deployments can strain personal relationships and disrupt a stable sense of self.

Discussing How Military Culture Contributes to Imposter Syndrome

Military culture, with its high standards and constant evaluation, significantly contributes to feelings of imposter syndrome among service members. Imposter syndrome is characterized by the internalized fear of being exposed as a "fraud," despite evident success and accomplishments. In the military, this phenomenon is exacerbated by several cultural factors.

Firstly, the military values excellence and competence, often setting high expectations for its members. The pressure to perform flawlessly and the constant scrutiny from superiors can lead to self-doubt, particularly when comparing oneself to peers who appear to excel effortlessly. This culture of comparison and competition can cause even highly capable individuals to question their worth and feel undeserving of their achievements.

Secondly, the military's emphasis on resilience and strength can discourage individuals from acknowledging their struggles or seeking help. The stigma associated with perceived weakness or failure can prevent service members from voicing their insecurities, thereby intensifying feelings of inadequacy.

Moreover, the nature of military training and operations often involves rapidly acquiring new skills and adapting to different roles. This necessity for quick mastery can leave individuals feeling unprepared and unqualified, further fueling imposter syndrome. The imposter phenomenon is particularly prevalent during significant career milestones, such as promotions or assuming command positions, where the increased responsibility heightens self-scrutiny.

In conclusion, the identity challenges and cultural dynamics within the United States Air Force create a unique environment where imposter syndrome can thrive. The high standards of performance, the pressure to exhibit unwavering resilience, and the ever-present comparisons among peers all contribute to this pervasive issue. Understanding these factors is crucial in addressing and mitigating the impacts of imposter syndrome on service members' mental health and overall well-being.

Service in the military can be a challenging and rewarding journey. From the moment individuals don their uniform, they are immersed in a culture that demands excellence, resilience, and unwavering dedication. However, underneath the surface of honor and duty, many service members grapple with a hidden adversary known as imposter syndrome.

Identity in the military is not a static concept, but rather a synthesis of military service and personal life. This duality presents a unique challenge, as service members must navigate the structured world of military protocols while also managing the complexities of civilian existence. It is within this dichotomy that seeds of doubt and insecurity can take hold.

Imposter syndrome within military contexts becomes deeply entrenched within the crucible of military culture. This culture, characterized by high standards and a ceaseless pursuit of excellence, fosters pride and a sense of belonging but also creates an environment where self-doubt can flourish.

From the moment they enlist, service members find themselves in an environment where performance is paramount. The military sets lofty expectations, demanding nothing short of perfection from its ranks. The pressure to excel, combined with constant evaluation by superiors, provides fertile ground for imposter syndrome to thrive. Despite their accomplishments, many service members fear being exposed as frauds and feel unworthy of their successes.

In the highly competitive atmosphere of the military, individuals frequently compare themselves to their peers, resulting in feelings of inadequacy and uncertainty about their abilities. Even those who have achieved great success may question whether they genuinely deserve their accolades.

Within the military, resilience is highly esteemed. Service members are taught to endure hardships without complaint and to persevere in the face of adversity. However, this emphasis on strength can conceal the struggles hidden beneath the surface. The stigma surrounding mental health issues and the fear of appearing weak often hinder service members from seeking the support they require. As a result, feelings of inadequacy persist in silence, perpetuating the cycle of imposter syndrome.

The stigma associated with mental health concerns in the military has significant consequences. Many service members worry that acknowledging their mental health struggles will harm their careers, reputation or jeopardize a security clearance. Consequently, they suffer in silence, avoiding assistance because they do not wish to be perceived as weak. While strength and resilience are crucial in the military, they also contribute to a culture that views vulnerability as a flaw. Within the military culture, the stigma associated with mental health challenges is a significant concern. Service members who struggle with anxiety, depression, PTSD, or other mental health issues are apprehensive about seeking help due to the potential negative impact on their careers. Regrettably, in the past especially while I was on active duty there have been instances of discrimination or exclusion against those who turn to mental health support within the military.

Furthermore, the belief that seeking assistance is a sign of weakness can cause service members to internalize their struggles. They may believe that they should be able to handle everything independently, further exacerbating their feelings of distress. Some may even convince themselves that they are the sole individuals facing difficulties, leading to further isolation.

The stigma surrounding mental health challenges also has an impact on leadership positions in the military. Commanders and supervisors, facing intense performance demands, may inadvertently contribute to the perpetuation of this stigma by not prioritizing the mental well-being of their subordinates. Consequently, service members are reluctant to share their struggles due to the fear of being perceived as liabilities.

To combat the stigma associated with mental health challenges, a collective effort is required from every member of the military. Leaders must set a positive example by openly recognizing the importance of mental well-being and actively encouraging service members to seek help. By normalizing discussions about mental health, leaders can establish an environment where individuals feel safe to disclose their struggles without fear of judgement.

Training programs aimed at enhancing mental health literacy among service members play a critical role in dismantling the stigma. These programs educate individuals on common mental health issues, the signs and symptoms to look out for, and the available support resources. By doing so, they empower service members to identify when they or their colleagues may be struggling and take proactive steps towards seeking assistance.

In addition to training programs, peer support networks within the military can also contribute significantly to dismantling stigma and fostering solidarity among service members facing mental health challenges. These networks create a sense of community and understanding among peers, establishing a safe space where individuals can share their experiences, seek guidance, and offer support to one another.

Ultimately, breaking down the stigma surrounding mental health challenges within the military necessitates a cultural shift that prioritizes compassion, empathy, and understanding. By cultivating an environment where service members feel supported and valued, the military can empower its personnel to confront imposter syndrome head-on and embrace their full potential, both professionally and personally. In the fast-paced realm of military operations, adaptability plays a crucial role for service members. Often, they must quickly acquire new skills and step into leadership positions with minimal preparation. While this agility demonstrates their resilience, it also fosters sentiments of impostor syndrome. The gravity of responsibility, particularly during significant career milestones, intensifies self-doubt and the fear of being exposed as fraudulent.

The pressure to perform at an exceptional level can be extremely overwhelming, especially during pivotal moments in one's career, such as promotions or assuming command positions. These transitional periods bring about heightened responsibilities and expectations, leading service members to question their own capabilities. Consequently, they may experience amplified feelings of impostor syndrome, apprehensive about being unveiled as impostors if they fail to meet expectations. Within the fast-paced and dynamic environment of the United States Military, service members are frequently thrust into leadership roles and entrusted with significant responsibilities without prior notice. Whether it involves leading a critical mission team or taking command of a squadron, the weight of responsibility can be daunting, particularly for those grappling with impostor syndrome.

One of the distinguishing aspects of military service is the imperative to quickly master and adapt. Service members often find themselves in situations where they must rapidly learn new skills, technologies, and protocols, often under high-pressure circumstances where failure is not an option. This constant pressure to excel can exacerbate feelings of inadequacy as service members may fear that they lack the knowledge or experience necessary for success. Advancement within the military entails greater duti es and expectations. Those who excel may be promoted to positions of higher authority, where they will lead larger teams, oversee more complex projects, and make critical decisions. While these opportunities highlight their skills, they can also trigger impostor syndrome, causing individuals to question their qualifications.

Assuming command of a unit or squadron represents a significant milestone for any service member. It signifies years of dedication and hard work, along with the responsibility to lead and inspire subordinates. However, many service members struggle with self-doubt and uncertainty when transitioning into a leadership role. They may wonder if they possess the necessary qualities to effectively guide their team.

For service members in combat or operational environments, the weight of responsibility is even greater. They must navigate a complex and unpredictable landscape, making split-second decisions with potentially life-or-death consequences. The stress and trauma of combat can contribute to feelings of inadequacy and self-doubt. Leadership is not about attaining perfection, but rather acknowledging limitations, soliciting input, and making decisions with humility and integrity. By embracing vulnerability and seeking assistance, service members can find empowerment in their roles and inspire others to do the same.

Support and guidance serve as powerful remedies for imposter syndrome. Service members ought to seek out mentors and colleagues who can provide guidance, perspective, and reassurance. By surrounding themselves with a supportive network, service members can cultivate the confidence needed to excel in their leadership positions and overcome imposter syndrome.

To combat imposter syndrome within the military, it is imperative to address the cultural dynamics that perpetuate it. This entails acknowledging the pressures of performance, eliminating the stigma associated with mental health, and offering support to service members as they navigate their identities. These measures are essential for establishing a culture characterized by authenticity and resilience.

The recognition of the intense pressures associated with performance is a pivotal first step. Service members must realize that these pressures are a natural consequence of the military's high standards. It is crucial for them to understand that feelings of inadequacy are not indicative of personal shortcomings, but rather a reflection of the demanding environment in which they operate.

Another critical step is dismantling the stigma surrounding mental health. Service members should be encouraged to seek assistance without fear of negative repercussions. This necessitates a cultural shift that emphasizes the importance of mental well-being and regards seeking support as an indication of strength rather than weakness.

Furthermore, it is imperative to provide support for service members as they navigate their identities. This includes providing access to mental health resources such as counseling and therapy, as well as establishing peer support networks where individuals can share experiences and seek advice from others who have faced similar challenges.

The battle against imposter syndrome within the United States Military persists. Through understanding and compassion, service members can navigate self-doubt and emerge stronger than ever. True strength within the military culture lies not in perfection, but in the bravery to confront vulnerabilities and embrace self-discovery. As the military evolves, its approach to supporting the mental health and overall well-being of its personnel must evolve as well.

CHAPTER 3

UPHOLDING EXCELLENCE
THE PRESSURE OF HIGH EXPECTATIONS

In the world of the military, excellence isn't just a goal; it's the standard. From the moment they enlist, military members are immersed in a culture that values precision, discipline, and unwavering commitment. But with that dedication comes a weighty burden – the pressure of high expectations.

From day one, recruits are taught that mediocrity is not an option. They undergo rigorous training, where attention to detail can mean the difference between success and failure, even life and death. Every task, no matter how small, is executed with precision. It's not just about completing the mission; it's about doing so flawlessly.

But this relentless pursuit of perfection can take its toll. The constant pressure to excel, coupled with the fear of falling short, can fuel feelings of inadequacy and self-doubt. Military members may find themselves grappling with imposter syndrome, questioning whether they truly measure up to the standards set by their peers and superiors.

The standards expected of military personnel are nothing short of extraordinary. Physical fitness must be maintained at peak levels, readiness for deployment must be unwavering, and decisions made in high-stakes situations must be swift and decisive. Anything less is simply not acceptable.

This environment of high expectations can contribute significantly to imposter syndrome among military personnel. Here are a few examples:

Comparisons with Peers

In the military, teamwork and solidarity are foundational principles. Service members work closely with their peers, often in high-pressure and high-stakes environments. While this fosters a sense of unity, it can also intensify the pressure to perform at a high level.

Imagine a scenario where a group of soldiers is training together for a mission. Each member of the team brings unique skills and experiences to the table, and they rely on one another to succeed. However, if one soldier perceives their peers as excelling in their roles while they struggle, it can trigger feelings of inadequacy and self-doubt.

This sense of comparison is heightened by the visible successes of others. When a peer receives praise or recognition for their accomplishments, it can serve as a constant reminder of one's own perceived shortcomings. The fear of not measuring up to these high-performing peers can create a sense of impostorism – the belief that one is not truly deserving of their position.

Not only this, but in a competitive environment like the military, there may be a reluctance to admit to struggling or seeking help.

Military members may fear being seen as weak or incompetent if they acknowledge their feelings of inadequacy. This can lead to a cycle of self-doubt, where individuals internalize their struggles rather than seeking support from their peers or superiors.

The pressure to compare oneself to others is further exacerbated by the hierarchical structure of the military. Rank and seniority are highly valued, and individuals may feel pressure to prove themselves worthy of advancement. This constant striving for validation and recognition can perpetuate feelings of impostorism, as individuals question whether they truly belong among their high-achieving peers.

Fear of Failure

In the military, failure is not an option. The stakes are incredibly high, and the consequences of mistakes can be severe, both for the individual and for their team. This environment fosters a fear of failure that can create a constant sense of pressure to perform perfectly, leading individuals to question whether they truly belong in their roles.

Consider a scenario where a service member is responsible for a critical task, such as coordinating a mission or managing equipment vital to the operation's success. The weight of this responsibility can be overwhelming. They know that even a small mistake could have far-reaching implications, potentially endangering lives or compromising the mission. This intense pressure to avoid failure can lead to significant stress and anxiety.

The fear of failure is not just about the immediate consequences; it also involves concerns about long-term impacts on one's career. Military personnel are acutely aware that their performance is continuously evaluated, and any perceived shortcomings can affect their chances for promotion, special assignments, or even continued service. This awareness can make individuals hyper-vigilant, always striving to prove their competence and worthiness.

the military culture often emphasizes toughness and resilience, leaving little room for admitting mistakes or seeking help. Service members might fear that acknowledging any shortcomings could be seen as a sign of weakness or incompetence, further fueling their imposter syndrome. They may internalize their fears, constantly questioning whether they are truly capable and deserving of their position.

Another aspect of this fear is the pressure to uphold the reputation of their unit and the military as a whole. Service members are part of a larger entity that prides itself on excellence and reliability. The fear of letting down their comrades or tarnishing the image of their unit can be a powerful motivator, but it can also exacerbate feelings of inadequacy and self-doubt.

For instance, a soldier tasked with leading a mission might obsess over every detail, fearing that a single oversight could lead to failure. This relentless self-scrutiny can erode their confidence, making them doubt their abilities even when they are performing well. The constant fear of failure can create a paralyzing effect, where the individual feels they must be perfect in every aspect of their role.

Perfectionism "A real story of a military solider"

Let's take a look at one Army soldier's experience, he states as a young non-MOS (Military Occupational Specialty) related soldier in an Infantry unit, highlighting how it challenged his sense of self-autonomy and understanding of military teamwork. Recalling past memories, he expressed a mix of hurt and intense anger due to being unaware of Imposter Syndrome and how his attempts to appease reinforced his perfectionist tendencies.

He described a continuous process of adapting to the customs and courtesies of each new unit. As a leader, there was constant pressure to perform exceptionally and surpass expectations, which became a mantra of tireless effort. This soldier often heard the phrase "Make it Happen," emphasizing the need to prove oneself repeatedly in new environments, starting from scratch until validation was earned.

He explained that he would consistently arrive early and stay late in new organizations, driven by a desire to learn and excel in the dominant MOS before feeling worthy. However, this dedication led to a diminishing sense of positive self-worth and self-reflection.

To manage these feelings, the soldier adopted a new perspective. He began appreciating every achievement as an experience worth embracing rather than merely a hurdle to overcome. This shift in mindset allowed him to regain control over his emotions and find value in every step of his journey.

Leadership Expectations:

Those in leadership positions within the military are held to particularly high standards. They are expected to make decisions quickly and decisively, often in high-pressure situations. The fear of making a wrong decision or being perceived as incompetent can contribute to imposter syndrome among military leaders.

Military leaders are often tasked with making decisions that can have immediate and profound consequences. Whether it's strategizing for a mission, managing the welfare of their troops, or responding to unforeseen challenges, the pressure to perform flawlessly is immense. The weight of these responsibilities can be overwhelming, leading leaders to question their own capabilities and judgment.

Consider a scenario where a military officer must make a rapid decision in a combat situation. The lives of their team members may depend on their ability to quickly assess the situation and act accordingly. The fear of making a mistake that could endanger their comrades can be paralyzing, causing the leader to doubt their decision-making abilities. This doubt can persist even if the leader has a strong track record of successful decisions, as the stakes are perpetually high.

Military culture places a strong emphasis on strength, resilience, and confidence. Leaders are expected to embody these qualities, often projecting an image of unwavering certainty. This expectation can make it difficult for leaders to admit to any self-doubt or seek support, as they may fear being perceived as weak or unfit for their role. The pressure to maintain this facade can exacerbate feelings of imposter syndrome, as leaders may feel they are constantly at risk of being "found out" as inadequate.

Perception of Weakness:

In the military, strength and resilience are highly prized qualities. Service members are trained to project confidence and capability, often under the most challenging conditions. This culture can make it difficult for individuals to admit to feelings of inadequacy or self-doubt, as such admissions are often perceived as signs of weakness.

The fear of being judged or ostracized for expressing vulnerability can lead many service members to internalize their struggles. Rather than seeking help, they may choose to suffer in silence, believing that acknowledging their doubts could undermine their credibility and respect among their peers and superiors. This internalization of struggles can exacerbate feelings of imposter syndrome, creating a cycle of self-doubt and isolation.

The expectation to maintain a strong facade can prevent open discussions about mental health and personal challenges. Service members might worry that revealing their insecurities could negatively impact their careers, leading to fewer opportunities for advancement or key assignments. This concern reinforces the stigma around seeking support, further entrenching the belief that one must handle their issues alone.

Drawing to the conclusion, the relentless pursuit of excellence in the military, while fostering a culture of high achievement and precision, also imposes a significant burden on service members. The constant pressure to meet extraordinary standards can fuel feelings of inadequacy and self-doubt, manifesting as imposter syndrome. Whether through comparisons with peers, fear of failure, or the struggle to translate military experience to civilian life, these pressures are ever-present and challenging.

Recognizing and addressing these feelings is crucial for the well-being of military personnel. By fostering an environment that values open communication, support, and the acknowledgment that perfection is an ideal rather than a requirement, the military can help mitigate the impact of imposter syndrome. Embracing the humanity behind the uniform, and understanding that even the most disciplined and capable individuals face moments of doubt, can lead to a more resilient and confident force.

CHAPTER 4

THE SHIFTING SANDS
TRANSITIONING ROLES IN SERVICE

In the military, change is a constant. Service members are frequently faced with transitioning between ranks, roles, and units, each shift bringing new challenges and expectations. These transitions, while integral to military life, can be disorienting and stressful, contributing to feelings of uncertainty and self-doubt.

Navigating these shifting sands requires adaptability and resilience, but it also takes a toll on mental well-being. Moving from one role to another or advancing in rank involves more than just new responsibilities; it demands a rapid adjustment to different expectations and environments. These changes can be particularly challenging because each role within the military has its own unique set of skills, behaviors, and standards.

When a service member is promoted, they often have to prove themselves all over again, not just to their superiors, but to their peers and subordinates. This pressure to perform can be intense. The individual might feel like they need to demonstrate their worth immediately, which can trigger feelings of imposter syndrome. They may start to question if they truly deserve their new position, or if they are capable of meeting the new expectations placed upon them.

Similarly, transferring to a new unit can be just as challenging. Every unit has its own culture and way of operating, and fitting into a new team can feel like starting from scratch. The service member might worry about being accepted by their new peers or living up to the reputation they built in their previous unit. These concerns can amplify feelings of inadequacy and self-doubt.

Highlighting the psychological impact of these transitions is crucial. Each role change or move to a new unit involves not just a shift in duties but also a significant adjustment period. The stress of these changes can lead to anxiety, reduced self-esteem, and an overwhelming sense of doubt about one's abilities. Understanding and addressing the psychological toll of these transitions can help erase the impact of imposter syndrome, ensuring that service members feel supported and valued through every stage of their military careers.

Challenges of transitioning between ranks, roles, and units

Transitioning between ranks, roles, and units in the military is a complex process fraught with challenges. Each change demands significant adjustments, both professionally and personally, and can impact a service member's sense of stability and confidence.

1. Transitioning Between Ranks

Advancing in rank is often seen as a milestone achievement, but it comes with its own set of pressures and uncertainties. When military members are promoted, they must quickly adapt to their new responsibilities, which are often more complex and carry greater consequences. This shift can be exhausting, as higher ranks typically involve leadership roles, requiring a service member to not only manage tasks but also mentor and oversee others.

One major challenge is the immediate need to prove oneself in the new role. A newly promoted officer or non-commissioned officer (NCO) might feel the pressure to demonstrate their capabilities from day one, aware that their performance is under scrutiny from both superiors and subordinates. This expectation can lead to heightened stress and anxiety, as the individual may fear making mistakes or not living up to the high standards associated with their new rank.

- **Heightened Responsibility and Decision-Making**

With higher rank comes increased responsibility and the need for decisive action. Newly promoted leaders are often required to make critical decisions that can have significant impacts on their unit's operations and the well-being of their team members. The weight of these decisions can be overwhelming, particularly for those who are still adjusting to their new role. The fear of making a wrong choice or failing to act swiftly enough can contribute to self-doubt and feelings of inadequacy.

- **Managing and Leading Others**

Leadership roles demand more than just technical proficiency; they require the ability to inspire, mentor, and guide others. A newly promoted service member must shift from being a peer to being a leader, which can be a challenging transition. They must navigate the delicate balance of maintaining respect and companionship while asserting authority and making tough calls. This dynamic can be particularly stressful if the leader feels unprepared or uncertain about their leadership abilities.

- **Perception and Expectations**

The perception of a leader's competence is critical in the military. Superiors expect new leaders to step into their roles seamlessly, while subordinates look to them for direction and confidence. This dual expectation can create a high-pressure environment where the leader feels they must constantly prove themselves. The fear of failing to meet these expectations can lead to imposter syndrome, where the individual doubts their own qualifications and fears being exposed as a fraud.

- **Adapting to New Skill Sets**

Each rank advancement often brings a need for new skills and knowledge. For example, transitioning from a technical specialist to a leadership role involves learning about personnel management, strategic planning, and conflict resolution—skills that may not have been emphasized in their previous position. This rapid acquisition of new competencies can be challenging, especially if the individual feels they must master these skills quickly to be effective in their new role.

- **Navigating Peer Dynamics**

Promotion can also alter relationships with former peers. A service member who is promoted within the same unit may find themselves leading individuals who were once their equals. This shift can create tension and require the new leader to establish clear boundaries and command respect without alienating their former peers. Managing these dynamics is crucial for maintaining unit cohesion and effectiveness, but it can also add to the stress and self-doubt experienced during the transition.

- **Support Systems and Mentorship**

Having a robust support system can make a significant difference in easing the transition to a higher rank. Mentorship from experienced leaders can provide valuable guidance and reassurance. However, not all service members have access to strong mentors, and those who don't may feel isolated in their new roles. Encouraging a culture of mentorship and support within the military can help new leaders feel more confident and less alone in their transition

2. Transitioning Between Roles

Shifting roles within the military often means stepping into unfamiliar territory. Even within the same rank, different roles can require vastly different skill sets and knowledge bases. For example, a military member might transition from a technical specialty to a leadership position, or from an operational role to a strategic planning role. Each of these changes requires a steep learning curve and the ability to adapt quickly.

- **Rapid Acquisition of New Skills and Knowledge**

One significant challenge in changing roles is the need to acquire new skills and knowledge rapidly. Each role in the military has its own set of requirements and expectations, which can be drastically different from previous positions held. For instance, moving from a technical role focused on specific tasks and expertise to a leadership role that requires managing personnel, making strategic decisions, and handling administrative duties can be overwhelming. The military member must quickly learn and master these new skills to perform effectively in their new position.

The pressure to become proficient quickly is intense. There is often little time for gradual learning or on-the-job training. The individual must show their competence immediately to maintain credibility and the confidence of their peers and superiors. This rapid learning process can lead to significant stress and anxiety, as the service member might fear falling short of the high standards expected in their new role.

- **Balancing Old and New Responsibilities**

Another challenge is balancing the learning curve of the new role while still managing existing responsibilities. Often, service members are not fully relieved of their previous duties while they transition to their new roles. This dual burden can lead to an increased workload and heightened stress levels. The individual must juggle learning and performing new tasks while ensuring that their old responsibilities do not suffer.

This balancing act can be particularly demanding if the service member's previous role was already high-pressure or time-consuming. The added responsibilities can stretch their capacity to manage effectively, leading to burnout and reduced performance in both roles. The fear of failing to meet expectations in either area can exacerbate feelings of inadequacy and imposter syndrome.

- **Adapting to New Expectations and Environments**

Each role within the military comes with its own set of expectations and operational environments. Transitioning to a new role often means adjusting to different leadership styles, team dynamics, and mission objectives. For example, moving from an operational role, which may involve direct action and immediate decision-making, to a strategic planning role, which requires long-term thinking and coordination, involves a significant shift in mindset and approach.

Adapting to these new expectations can be challenging. The military member must quickly learn to adjust into the new environment and understand the specific goals and priorities of their role. This adaptation process can be stressful, particularly if the new role feels vastly different from previous experiences. The individual may worry about their ability to meet the new demands and whether they can adapt quickly enough to be effective.

- **Internal and External Perceptions**

Transitioning to a new role also involves managing both internal and external perceptions. Internally, the service member may fight with self-doubt and question their ability to succeed in their new position. Externally, they must prove their competence and earn the trust and respect of their new colleagues and superiors. This dual challenge can intensify the pressure to perform and lead to heightened levels of stress and anxiety.

The fear of being perceived as incompetent or not up to the task can contribute to imposter syndrome. The individual might feel like they are constantly under the radar, which can undermine their confidence and affect their ability to fully accept their new role. Building confidence and competence in the new position takes time, but the immediate need to establish credibility can make the transition period particularly difficult.

3. Transitioning Between Units

Moving to a new unit presents its own unique set of challenges. Each unit in the military has its own culture, norms, and operating procedures. Integrating into a new unit means learning these nuances while trying to establish oneself as a competent and reliable member of the team.

- **Social and Cultural Adaptation**

A primary challenge of transitioning to a new unit is the social and cultural adaptation required. Each unit has its own unique dynamics and established norms that newcomers must quickly learn to navigate. This includes understanding the informal rules, communication styles, and interpersonal relationships that define the unit's culture. For example, a unit that emphasizes teamwork and collective decision-making might require a different approach than one that values individual initiative and competition.

Newcomers must build trust with their new colleagues, which can be a delicate process. Trust is not given automatically; it must be earned through consistent actions and demonstrated competence. This need to prove oneself can be stressful, especially when trying to fit into an established group with its own history and shared experiences. The pressure to integrate smoothly and be accepted by the new team can lead to feelings of isolation and uncertainty, particularly if the newcomer's previous unit had a markedly different environment.

- **Loss of Support Network**

Another significant challenge is the loss of the support network built in the previous unit. Over time, military members develop strong bonds and a deep sense of companionship with their peers. These relationships provide emotional support, guidance, and a sense of belonging. When transitioning to a new unit, these connections do not automatically transfer. The military member must start from scratch to develop similar bonds, which can take considerable time and effort.

During this period of adjustment, feelings of loneliness and self-doubt can intensify. The absence of familiar faces and trusted allies can make the individual feel isolated and unsure of their place in the new unit. This lack of a support system can intensify the stress of adapting to a new environment and contribute to imposter syndrome, as the service member might question their ability to fit in and succeed.

- **Learning New Procedures and Expectations**

Every unit operates with its own set of procedures and expectations. Transitioning to a new unit involves quickly learning these new protocols to ensure smooth integration. This can include everything from different training routines to unique operational strategies. The need to adapt swiftly to these new ways of doing things can be overwhelming, particularly if the military member feels pressured to demonstrate immediate competence.

Moreover, the formal expectations of the new unit may differ from those of the previous one. A military member who excelled in one unit's operational style might find themselves struggling to adjust to a completely different set of standards and practices. This can lead to frustration and self-doubt, as the individual might feel their previous skills and experiences are not adequately valued or applicable in the new context.

- **Navigating Group Dynamics**

Integrating into a new unit also requires navigating existing group dynamics. Established units have their own internal hierarchies, alliances, and social structures. Newcomers must carefully observe and understand these dynamics to find their place within the group. Missteps or misunderstandings can affect the integration process and create additional stress.

For example, a military member might inadvertently step on toes by challenging an established leader or by failing to recognize an informal but influential member of the unit. These social faux pas can make it more difficult to build trust and be accepted, further fueling feelings of inadequacy and self-doubt.

The challenges of transitioning between ranks, roles, and units in the military are significant and complex. Each change requires a quick adaptation to new responsibilities, environments, and expectations, which can strain even the most resilient individuals. The pressure to prove oneself in a new position, the need to quickly acquire new skills, and the loss of established support networks can all contribute to stress, anxiety, and feelings of inadequacy.

Understanding the psychological impact of these transitions is crucial for supporting service members. Acknowledging the difficulties they face and providing robust support systems, including mentorship and resources for mental health, can help ease these transitions. By creating an environment where military members feel supported and valued, the military can help reduce the effects of imposter syndrome and ensure that its personnel are confident and capable in their evolving roles.

Recognizing that each transition is an opportunity for growth and development, rather than solely a source of stress, can also shift perspectives. By focusing on the skills gained and the resilience built through these experiences, service members can better navigate the shifting sands of their careers. Ultimately, supporting service members through these transitions not only enhances their well-being but also strengthens the military as a whole.

CHAPTER 5

IN THE SHADOWS COMPARING AGAINST PEERS

In the tight-knit world of the military, service members constantly find themselves shoulder to shoulder with their peers. This close proximity promotes a strong sense of unity and teamwork, but it also breeds an environment ripe for comparison. The phenomenon of comparing oneself to others is a pervasive aspect of military life, where the achievements and abilities of fellow service members are always on display.

From basic training to advanced deployments, every step of a service member's career is marked by assessments, evaluations, and visible benchmarks of success. These metrics, designed to ensure readiness and excellence, inadvertently fuel the tendency to measure one's own worth against that of others. Whether it's physical fitness scores, leadership evaluations, or mission performance, the pressure to keep up with or surpass peers is relentless.

This culture of comparison can have a significant impact on mental well-being and self-esteem. Constantly measuring oneself against others can lead to feelings of inadequacy and self-doubt. Even highly capable service members might begin to question their own abilities and worth if they perceive themselves as falling short compared to their peers. This internalized pressure can erode confidence and contribute to stress, anxiety, and imposter syndrome.

Also, the impact of comparison extends beyond individual self-perception. It can strain relationships within units, as service members might feel competitive rather than collaborative. The stress of trying to measure up can create a sense of isolation, as individuals may be reluctant to seek support or admit to struggles for fear of appearing weak. Understanding and addressing the phenomenon of comparison is crucial for fostering a supportive and healthy environment within the military, where service members can thrive without constantly feeling overshadowed by their peers.

Comparison Among Service Members

The phenomenon of comparison among service members is deeply ingrained in military culture. From the earliest days of basic training, individuals are placed in environments where their performance is constantly measured against that of their peers. This competitive atmosphere is intended to motivate and push service members to achieve their best, but it also sets the stage for ongoing comparisons that can have complex psychological effects.

Competitive Training Environment

Basic training is designed to be a rigorous, high-pressure environment where recruits must prove themselves. This setting naturally fosters competition. Physical fitness tests, marksmanship scores, and field exercises all provide clear metrics that recruits can use to compare their performance against that of their peers. Those who excel are often recognized and rewarded, which reinforces the idea that comparison is a key component of success.

However, this constant comparison can have negative effects on those who perceive themselves as lagging behind. Recruits who struggle with certain aspects of training may begin to see themselves as less capable or less worthy, leading to a decline in self-esteem and confidence. The intense focus on competition can also overshadow the importance of personal growth and teamwork.

Evaluation and Promotion

As service members advance in their careers, the comparisons continue. Performance evaluations, promotion boards, and commendation systems all contribute to a culture where individuals are measured against one another. These assessments are necessary to maintain high standards and ensure that the most capable individuals are placed in positions of responsibility. However, they also perpetuate the cycle of comparison.

Military members are acutely aware of how their evaluations compare to those of their peers. A lower rating or a missed promotion can be demoralizing, leading individuals to question their abilities and worth. Even those who perform well may feel pressure to continually outperform their peers, creating a constant sense of competition and stress.

Physical Fitness Standards

Physical fitness is a critical component of military readiness, and maintaining high fitness standards is essential. Regular fitness tests and evaluations provide tangible benchmarks that military members can use to gauge their performance. While these standards are necessary, they also serve as another point of comparison.

Military members who excel in physical fitness often receive recognition and respect from their peers, reinforcing the importance of these comparisons. Conversely, those who struggle with fitness standards may feel inadequate or embarrassed, particularly if they perceive themselves as less capable than their peers. This can lead to feelings of shame and self-doubt, which can undermine overall morale and mental well-being.

Mission Performance and Operational Success

Operational success and mission performance are perhaps the most significant areas where comparison occurs. Military members are frequently assessed based on their contributions to mission outcomes, and those who demonstrate exceptional skill and leadership are often recognized and rewarded. These comparisons can be particularly intense in high-stakes environments, where the consequences of failure are severe.

While recognizing and rewarding excellence is important, it can also create an environment where individuals feel pressured to constantly outperform their peers. The fear of making mistakes or falling short can lead to increased stress and anxiety. Additionally, comparing oneself to highly successful peers can create feelings of inadequacy and imposter syndrome, even among those who are otherwise competent and capable.

Peer Dynamics and Social Comparison

The close-knit nature of military units means that service members spend a great deal of time together, both professionally and socially. This proximity can intensify the tendency to compare oneself to others. Social comparison theory suggests that individuals evaluate their own abilities and worth by comparing themselves to others, and this dynamic is particularly pronounced in the military.

Service members might compare themselves to their peers in terms of skills, accomplishments, and even personal qualities. This constant comparison can lead to feelings of envy, resentment, and inadequacy. It can also strain relationships within the unit, as individuals might feel competitive rather than collaborative. The pressure to measure up can create a sense of isolation, as service members may be reluctant to share their struggles or seek support.

Impact of Comparison on Mental Health

The constant comparison among service members can significantly impact their mental well-being and self-esteem. This culture of comparison can lead to a range of negative psychological outcomes, including stress, anxiety, depression, and imposter syndrome. Understanding these impacts is essential for creating a supportive environment that promotes mental health and resilience.

Stress and Anxiety

One of the most immediate effects of constant comparison is increased stress and anxiety. Military members are often aware that their performance is being measured against that of their peers, creating a high-pressure environment. The need to continually prove oneself can lead to chronic stress, which affects both mental and physical health.

The stress of comparison can manifest in various ways. Some military members might experience heightened anxiety before evaluations or fitness tests, fearing that they will not measure up. This anxiety can interfere with performance, creating a vicious cycle where fear of failure leads to actual failure, which in turn reinforces feelings of inadequacy.

Depression and Low Self-Esteem

Persistent comparison can erode self-esteem and lead to depression. When service members perceive themselves as less capable or successful than their peers, they may develop a negative self-image. This negative self-perception can be particularly damaging if it becomes internalized, leading individuals to believe that they are inherently less valuable or competent.

Low self-esteem can have far-reaching effects on a military member's mental health and overall well-being. It can decrease motivation, hinder performance, and lead to withdrawal from social and professional activities. Over time, these feelings of worthlessness and inadequacy can contribute to the development of depression, further impacting the individual's ability to function effectively.

Relationship Strain and Isolation

The competitive environment created by constant comparison can strain relationships within units. Military members might feel envious or resentful of their peers' successes, leading to interpersonal conflicts. This competitive atmosphere can undermine the sense of mutual support that is crucial for effective teamwork.

Also, individuals who feel they do not measure up to their peers may withdraw socially, leading to feelings of isolation. They might be reluctant to share their struggles or seek help, fearing judgment or rejection. This isolation can exacerbate feelings of inadequacy and contribute to mental health issues such as depression and anxiety.

Reduced Performance and Career Progression

The psychological impact of comparison can also affect performance and career progression. Military members who struggle with low self-esteem or imposter syndrome may be less likely to take on challenging assignments or pursue leadership roles. Their fear of failure can lead to missed opportunities and hinder career advancement.

Furthermore, the stress and anxiety associated with comparison can negatively impact cognitive functioning and decision-making abilities. Service members might experience difficulty concentrating, making it harder to perform effectively in high-pressure situations. This reduced performance can reinforce feelings of inadequacy, creating a feedback loop that further undermines self-esteem and mental well-being.

The phenomenon of comparison among service members, though rooted in military culture, poses significant challenges to mental well-being and self-esteem. The constant need to measure up to peers can lead to chronic stress, anxiety, and a host of other psychological issues. This high-pressure environment, while driving excellence, also creates an atmosphere where self-doubt and feelings of inadequacy can grow.

Understanding the impact of comparison is crucial for creating a healthier, more supportive military culture. By acknowledging the pressures military members face and implementing measures to mitigate these stressors, the military can help individuals maintain their mental health and self-esteem. This might include promoting a more collaborative environment, providing mental health resources, and encouraging open communication about the struggles associated with comparison.

Finally, addressing the issues related to comparison among peers not only benefits the individual service members but also strengthens the overall effectiveness and cohesion of military units. By promoting a culture that values personal growth, resilience, and mutual support, the military can ensure that its members thrive both personally and professionally.

CHAPTER 6

BEHIND THE FAÇADE
MASKING VULNERABILITY

In the demanding and disciplined world of the military, the facade of strength and resilience is often a necessary mask. Service members are trained to project confidence and competence, embodying the ideals of bravery and fortitude. Yet, beneath this exterior, many struggle with feelings of inadequacy and vulnerability. The pressure to conform to the image of the unshakeable warrior can make it difficult for individuals to acknowledge and express their true emotions, leading to a pervasive tendency to hide their struggles.

From the moment they enter the military, service members are taught to prioritize mission success and the well-being of their unit above all else. This training, while essential for operational effectiveness, can also discourage the open expression of personal challenges. Admitting to feelings of self-doubt or seeking help is often seen as a sign of weakness, something that could potentially undermine trust and cohesion within a unit. As a result, many service members put on a brave face, masking their internal struggles to maintain the facade of strength.

This tendency to hide vulnerability has deep roots in military culture, where stoicism and emotional control are highly valued. However, the constant suppression of genuine feelings can take a significant toll on mental health. Service members may feel isolated, believing they are the only ones grappling with these issues. This isolation can exacerbate feelings of imposter syndrome, as individuals become convinced that their peers are effortlessly meeting the high standards expected of them.

Understanding the importance of authenticity and vulnerability is crucial in overcoming imposter syndrome. By creating an environment where military members feel safe to express their true feelings, the military can help individuals build resilience and confidence. Encouraging authenticity not only supports mental well-being but also fosters deeper connections within units, enhancing overall cohesion and effectiveness.

In this chapter, we will explore the common tendency among service members to hide their feelings of inadequacy and vulnerability. We will discuss how this behavior perpetuates imposter syndrome and examine the benefits of embracing authenticity. By shining a light on the importance of vulnerability, we aim to uncover the path to a healthier, more supportive military culture.

Tendency to Hide Feelings of Inadequacy and Vulnerability

In the military, the expectation to embody strength, competence, and resilience is paramount. From basic training onward, service members are instilled with the ethos of unwavering fortitude, often at the expense of acknowledging and addressing their own vulnerabilities. This deeply ingrained cultural norm can lead to a widespread tendency to hide feelings of inadequacy and vulnerability, perpetuating a cycle of emotional suppression and internal struggle.

Cultural Expectations and Stoicism

Military culture places a high value on stoicism and emotional control. Service members are taught to manage their emotions, maintain composure under pressure, and prioritize mission success above all else. This training is essential for operational effectiveness, especially in high-stress and high-stakes environments where clear-headed decision-making is crucial. However, it also creates an environment where expressing vulnerability is often seen as a liability rather than a strength.

The stigma surrounding vulnerability in the military context can be significant. Admitting to feelings of self-doubt or seeking help for emotional struggles is frequently perceived as a sign of weakness. This perception can discourage service members from openly discussing their internal challenges, leading them to mask their true feelings behind a facade of confidence and competence.

Impact on Mental Health

The act of hiding feelings of inadequacy and vulnerability can have significant negative impacts on mental health. Military members may experience intense internal conflict, as they struggle to reconcile their public persona with their private feelings of self-doubt. This dissonance can lead to chronic stress, anxiety, and depression, as individuals feel increasingly isolated and misunderstood.

Suppressing emotions can also promote feelings of imposter syndrome. When service members perceive that their peers are effortlessly meeting the high standards expected of them, they may begin to believe that they are the only ones struggling. This belief reinforces the notion that they are not truly capable or deserving of their role, deepening their sense of inadequacy and isolation.

Social and Professional Consequences

The tendency to hide vulnerability can also affect social dynamics within military units. Service members who feel compelled to project an image of unwavering strength may struggle to form genuine connections with their peers. This lack of authenticity can hinder the development of trust and camaraderie, essential elements for effective teamwork and unit cohesion.

Professionally, the fear of being perceived as weak or incompetent can prevent military members from seeking necessary support or mentoring. This reluctance to ask for help can impede personal and professional growth, as individuals may miss out on valuable opportunities for learning and development. Over time, the cumulative effect of these missed opportunities can hinder career progression and overall job satisfaction.

Reinforcement of the Facade

The military's hierarchical structure can reinforce the tendency to hide vulnerability. Junior service members often look to their superiors for cues on acceptable behavior. When leaders consistently project an image of infallibility, it sends a message that vulnerability is not permissible. This dynamic creates a self-reinforcing cycle, where each level of the hierarchy feels compelled to maintain the facade of strength, perpetuating the culture of emotional suppression.

Breaking the Cycle

Breaking the cycle of hiding vulnerability requires a cultural shift within the military. Leaders at all levels must model and promote the value of authenticity and emotional openness. By sharing their own experiences with vulnerability and encouraging open dialogue about mental health, leaders can create an environment where service members feel safe to express their true feelings without fear of judgment or reprisal.

Importance of Authenticity and Vulnerability in Overcoming Imposter Syndrome

Addressing imposter syndrome within the military requires a fundamental shift towards embracing authenticity and vulnerability. While the culture of strength and stoicism has its place in ensuring operational success, creating an environment where service members can openly express their true selves is crucial for their mental well-being and overall effectiveness. By promoting authenticity and vulnerability, the military can help individuals overcome imposter syndrome and build a more resilient and cohesive force.

Building Trust

Authenticity and vulnerability are essential for building trust within military units. When service members feel safe to share their true feelings and experiences, it fosters a sense of mutual understanding and support. Open communication about struggles and challenges helps to break down the barriers of isolation that imposter syndrome can create. Knowing that their peers also face similar doubts and fears can alleviate feelings of inadequacy and promote a sense of belonging.

Leaders play a critical role in this process. When leaders model vulnerability by sharing their own experiences with self-doubt and failure, it sets a powerful example for their subordinates. It demonstrates that vulnerability is not a weakness but a strength, and it encourages others to be more open about their own struggles. This transparency helps to create an environment of psychological safety, where service members feel comfortable seeking support and discussing their challenges.

Enhancing Personal Growth and Development

Embracing authenticity and vulnerability can significantly enhance personal growth and development. When service members are honest about their strengths and weaknesses, they can more effectively identify areas for improvement and seek out opportunities for growth. Acknowledging and addressing gaps in knowledge or skills, rather than hiding them, allows for targeted development and training, leading to increased competence and confidence over time.

This approach also encourages a growth mindset, where service members view challenges and failures as opportunities for learning rather than as threats to their self-worth. By reframing setbacks in this way, individuals can develop greater resilience and adaptability, which are crucial qualities for both personal and professional success in the military.

Reducing Stress and Anxiety

Authenticity and vulnerability can help reduce the stress and anxiety associated with imposter syndrome. When military members no longer feel the need to maintain a facade of perfection, they experience less pressure to conform to unrealistic expectations. This reduction in stress can lead to improved mental health and well-being, as individuals are freed from the constant fear of being exposed as frauds.

Furthermore, open discussions about mental health and the normalcy of experiencing self-doubt can destigmatize these issues and encourage more service members to seek help when needed. Access to mental health resources and support systems becomes more effective when individuals feel that their struggles are understood and accepted rather than judged.

Strengthening Leadership and Decision-Making

Vulnerability is also a critical component of effective leadership. Leaders who demonstrate authenticity and openness are more approachable and relatable, which can inspire greater loyalty and trust from their subordinates. These leaders are better equipped to make informed decisions, as they are more likely to seek input and feedback from their teams. This inclusive approach to leadership fosters a collaborative environment where diverse perspectives are valued, leading to better outcomes.

Additionally, leaders who are open about their own challenges and uncertainties can create a culture of continuous improvement, where mistakes are seen as opportunities for learning rather than as failures. This mindset encourages innovation and adaptability, which are essential for maintaining operational readiness in a rapidly changing environment.

Promoting Long-Term Resilience

In the long term, fostering authenticity and vulnerability can lead to a more resilient military force. Military members who feel supported and understood are more likely to stay committed to their roles and maintain high levels of performance. This resilience extends beyond individual well-being to the overall health of the unit, as cohesive and supportive teams are better equipped to handle the stresses and demands of military life.

By prioritizing authenticity and vulnerability, the military can create a culture where imposter syndrome is less likely to take root. Service members can develop a strong sense of self-worth and confidence in their abilities, grounded in a realistic understanding of their strengths and areas for growth. This foundation enables them to meet challenges head-on and contribute more effectively to their missions.

The journey to overcoming imposter syndrome in the military hinges on the willingness to embrace authenticity and vulnerability. While the culture of strength and stoicism is deeply rooted, creating space for genuine expression and emotional openness is essential for the mental well-being and overall effectiveness of service members. By having an environment where individuals feel safe to share their true feelings and experiences, the military can break down the barriers of isolation and self-doubt that imposter syndrome creates.

Leaders play a pivotal role in this transformation. When they model vulnerability and authenticity, they set a powerful example that encourages others to follow suit. This openness builds trust within units but also enhances personal growth and development, reduces stress and anxiety, and strengthens leadership and decision-making.

In the long run, prioritizing authenticity and vulnerability promotes a resilient and cohesive military force. Military members who feel supported and understood are better equipped to face the challenges of military life and contribute more effectively to their missions. By addressing imposter syndrome through these values, the military can cultivate a culture of continuous improvement, mutual support, and enduring strength.

CHAPTER 7

BATTLING THE INNER CRITIC
STRATEGIES FOR SELF-COMPASSION

In the high-stakes world of the military, service members are often their own harshest critics. The relentless drive for excellence, combined with the pressure to meet stringent standards, can lead to a persistent inner critic that magnifies every perceived flaw and failure. This inner voice, while intended to motivate and push individuals toward their best, can become a formidable adversary, fueling self-doubt and imposter syndrome. To counter this, cultivating self-compassion and self-acceptance becomes essential. These practices not only improve mental well-being but also enhance resilience and overall performance.

Imagine a seasoned soldier, Alex, who has served in multiple deployments and earned numerous commendations. Despite a record of excellence, Alex finds himself haunted by a recent mistake during a training exercise. The error was minor and quickly corrected, but Alex's inner critic seizes upon it, casting doubt on his competence and worthiness. Instead of acknowledging his extensive experience and contributions, Alex fixates on this single incident, allowing it to overshadow his many achievements.

This scenario is all too common among military members. The inner critic can be relentless, turning even minor setbacks into overwhelming sources of self-doubt. It whispers that they are not good enough, that their successes are mere flukes, and that they are bound to be exposed as frauds. This negative self-talk can erode confidence, making it difficult to perform at one's best and diminishing overall morale.

Enter the concept of self-compassion. Unlike self-criticism, which focuses on faults and shortcomings, self-compassion involves treating oneself with the same kindness and understanding that one would offer a friend. It's about recognizing that everyone makes mistakes, that imperfection is part of the human experience, and that these missteps do not define one's worth. For service members like Alex, learning to practice self-compassion can be transformative, helping to silence the inner critic and foster a more balanced, positive self-view.

Consider another scenario: Jamie, a junior officer, struggles with feelings of inadequacy. Despite receiving positive feedback from superiors and peers, Jamie's inner critic constantly undermines her achievements. She feels like an imposter, certain that her success is due to luck rather than skill. When Jamie begins to explore self-compassion, she starts by acknowledging her feelings of self-doubt without judgment. She reminds herself that many of her peers likely experience similar thoughts and that it's okay to not have all the answers. Gradually, Jamie learns to be kinder to herself, appreciating her efforts and recognizing her growth, even when things don't go perfectly.

Self-compassion doesn't mean lowering standards or becoming complacent. Instead, it's about creating a healthy, realistic relationship with oneself, where mistakes are seen as opportunities for learning rather than evidence of unworthiness. It encourages military members to balance the drive for excellence with the need for self-care, creating a more sustainable approach to personal and professional growth.

In this chapter, we will delve into practical strategies for cultivating self-compassion and self-acceptance. By adopting these practices, service members can learn to quiet their inner critics, build resilience, and approach their roles with greater confidence and clarity. Through real-life scenarios and actionable advice, we aim to equip readers with the tools they need to adopt their imperfections and thrive in their military careers.

Practical Strategies for Cultivating Self-Compassion and Self-Acceptance

Cultivating self-compassion and self-acceptance is a journey that involves changing deeply ingrained habits of self-criticism and judgment. Here are practical strategies to help service members foster a kinder, more accepting relationship with themselves.

1. Mindful Awareness

Mindful awareness is the cornerstone of self-compassion, helping individuals recognize and address their inner critic. It involves paying attention to thoughts and feelings without judgment, fostering a deeper understanding of one's mental state and its impact on well-being.

How to Practice:

Daily Check-In: Set aside a few minutes each day to sit quietly and observe your thoughts. Allow yourself to notice any critical or judgmental thoughts that arise without attempting to change them.

Simply acknowledge their presence and let them pass, creating a habit of non-judgmental awareness.

Mindful Breathing: Focus your attention on your breath. Inhale deeply through your nose and exhale slowly through your mouth. When your mind inevitably wanders to self-critical thoughts, gently redirect your focus back to your breathing. This practice helps anchor your attention and calms the mind.

Body Scan: Conduct a slow, deliberate scan of your body from head to toe. Pay attention to areas of tension or discomfort, acknowledging these sensations with kindness and curiosity. Instead of criticizing yourself for feeling tense or uncomfortable, accept these sensations as part of your current experience, promoting a compassionate connection with your body.

By integrating these practices into your daily routine, you can cultivate greater self-awareness and reduce the negative impact of your inner critic.

2. Self-Kindness

Self-kindness means treating yourself with the same care and compassion that you would offer to a close friend. Instead of harshly judging yourself for perceived shortcomings, respond with understanding and encouragement, promoting a more positive and supportive inner dialogue.

How to Practice:

Supportive Self-Talk: When you catch yourself engaging in self-criticism, pause and reframe your thoughts. Consider what you would say to a friend in a similar situation. For example, if you find yourself thinking, "I'm such a failure," try replacing it with, "I did my best, and it's okay to make mistakes." This shift in perspective can help soften self-judgment and promote a more compassionate inner voice. Regularly practice this reframing to build a habit of supportive self-talk.

Write a Compassionate Letter: Take some time to write a letter to yourself from the perspective of a supportive friend. Highlight your strengths, acknowledge your efforts, and offer comforting words for your struggles. For instance, you might write, "I know you're going through a tough time, but remember how strong and capable you are. You've overcome challenges before, and you can do it again." Keep this letter and read it whenever you need a reminder of your worth and resilience.

Acts of Kindness: Engage in small acts of kindness for yourself regularly. This could be taking a relaxing bath, enjoying a favorite hobby, or giving yourself permission to rest without guilt. Prioritize activities that bring you joy and relaxation, reinforcing the idea that you deserve care and compassion. For example, if you enjoy reading, set aside time each day to read a book purely for pleasure, or if you love nature, plan a regular walk in the park to rejuvenate your spirit.

By incorporating these practices into your daily life, you can cultivate a habit of self-kindness that counteracts the harshness of self-criticism and promotes a more compassionate and supportive relationship with yourself.

3. Common Humanity

Recognizing that everyone experiences difficulties and imperfections is essential for self-compassion. Understanding that you are not alone in your struggles can help diminish feelings of isolation and self-doubt.

How to Practice:

Shared Experiences: Engage in conversations with peers or colleagues about your challenges. By sharing your experiences, you can realize that others face similar issues. For example, discussing a recent mistake in a training exercise can reveal that many have faced similar setbacks, normalizing these experiences and fostering a sense of solidarity.

Group Support: Join a support group or community where members discuss and support each other through their difficulties. This could be a formal group like a military support circle or an informal gathering of friends. Such environments provide a safe space to share vulnerabilities and receive encouragement, reinforcing the idea that you are not alone.

Perspective Taking: Regularly remind yourself that making mistakes and facing challenges is part of the human experience. Reflect on stories of others who have overcome similar obstacles. For instance, reading about a highly respected leader who faced and overcame failures can provide perspective and inspiration, helping you see that struggles are a natural part of growth and success.

By incorporating these practices, you can foster a sense of common humanity, reducing feelings of isolation and enhancing your self-compassion.

4. Balancing Self-Improvement with Self-Acceptance

While striving for self-improvement is important, it should be balanced with self-acceptance. Accepting yourself as you are does not mean giving up on growth but recognizing your inherent worthiness regardless of achievements.

How to Practice:

Set Realistic Goals: Establish goals that are challenging yet achievable. Focus on incremental progress rather than perfection. Celebrate each milestone, no matter how small, to acknowledge your efforts and growth. For instance, if you're working on physical fitness, celebrate each improvement in your workout routine rather than just the end goal.

Progress Journaling: Keep a journal to document your progress and achievements. Reflect regularly on both your successes and the lessons learned from setbacks. This practice helps you see your growth over time and understand that setbacks are part of the journey. For example, note down how overcoming a challenge has made you more resilient or knowledgeable.

Self-Reflection: Dedicate time to reflect on your values, strengths, and the qualities that make you unique and valuable. Regularly acknowledging these aspects helps reinforce self-acceptance. For instance, if you value kindness, reflect on moments when you acted kindly and how that aligns with your self-worth.

By integrating these practices, you can maintain a healthy balance between striving for improvement and accepting yourself as you are, fostering both personal growth and a sense of inherent worthiness.

5. Seeking Professional Help

Sometimes, the inner critic can be deeply entrenched, making professional help beneficial. Therapists and counselors can provide strategies and support for cultivating self-compassion.

How to Practice:

Therapy: Consider therapy options such as Cognitive Behavioral Therapy (CBT) or Compassion-Focused Therapy (CFT). CBT helps identify and challenge negative thought patterns, replacing them with healthier ones. CFT specifically targets self-criticism and fosters a compassionate mindset. A therapist trained in these approaches can guide you through exercises and techniques to build self-compassion and diminish the power of your inner critic.

Workshops and Programs: Look for workshops, seminars, or online programs that focus on self-compassion and emotional resilience. These programs often provide structured activities, group discussions, and expert insights that can help you develop new coping strategies and perspectives. Many organizations, including military support networks, offer these resources to help service members enhance their emotional well-being.

Peer Counseling: Engage with peer counseling programs within the military. These programs connect you with someone who has faced similar experiences and challenges. Peer counselors provide empathetic support and practical advice from a place of understanding. Sharing your struggles with someone who truly understands your unique experiences can be incredibly validating and can help you feel less isolated.

By seeking professional help, you can access tailored support and effective strategies to overcome the inner critic, fostering greater self-compassion and overall mental well-being.

Cultivating self-compassion and self-acceptance is important for anyone battling an inner critic, particularly for those in high-pressure environments like the military. By observing mindful awareness, self-kindness, and recognizing our shared human experiences, military members can begin to quiet their inner critic and foster a healthier self-view. Balancing self-improvement with self-acceptance ensures that growth does not come at the cost of self-worth. Finally, seeking professional help when needed can provide additional support and strategies to solidify these practices.

As service members learn to extend the same compassion to themselves that they readily offer to others, they can build resilience, enhance their mental well-being, and more effectively navigate the challenges they face. The journey towards self-compassion is ongoing, but with these strategies, it becomes a feasible and rewarding path.

CHAPTER 8

THE POWER OF CONNECTION
SEEKING SUPPORT AND COMMUNITY

In the journey to overcome imposter syndrome, the power of connection cannot be overstated. Human beings are inherently social creatures, and the bonds we form with others can be an important source of strength and resilience. In the military, where the pressures and expectations are exceptionally high, seeking support from peers, mentors, and mental health professionals is not just beneficial—it's essential.

The importance of seeking support from various sources cannot be overstated. Peers who understand the unique challenges of military life can offer empathy and validation, helping individuals feel less isolated in their struggles. Mentors provide guidance and perspective, drawing on their own experiences to offer invaluable advice. Mental health professionals bring a wealth of knowledge and techniques to address the psychological aspects of imposter syndrome, helping service members develop healthier ways of thinking and coping.

Moreover, the sense of community and camaraderie within the military can play a pivotal role in overcoming imposter syndrome. Strong connections with fellow service members creates a sense of belonging and mutual support. This solidarity can diminish feelings of inadequacy and self-doubt, as individuals recognize that they are not alone in their experiences. Whether through formal support groups or informal gatherings, the bonds formed within the military community provide a powerful antidote to the isolation that imposter syndrome can create.

In this chapter, we will delve into the various avenues for seeking support and the significant impact that community and camaraderie can have on mental well-being. By exploring these connections, military members can find the strength to confront their inner critics and embrace their worth and achievements.

Importance of Support from Peers, Mentors, and Mental Health Professionals:

Seeking support from peers, mentors, and mental health professionals is crucial for overcoming imposter syndrome. Each of these sources offers unique benefits that contribute to a comprehensive support system.

Peers:

Peers play a significant role in providing emotional support and validation. Sharing experiences with those who face similar challenges can help normalize feelings of inadequacy and reduce the sense of isolation that imposter syndrome often brings. In the military, peers understand the unique pressures and expectations, making their support particularly resonant.

How Peers Help:

Shared Experiences:

Peers have firsthand knowledge of the military environment, making their insights and advice highly relevant. They understand the unique challenges and pressures that come with military service because they live through them daily. This shared experience creates a strong sense of camaraderie and trust, as there is an unspoken understanding of what each person is going through. For instance, when a service member discusses the stress of preparing for a deployment, their peers can relate to that anxiety and offer support based on their own experiences. This shared understanding helps to validate feelings and reduce the sense of isolation that often accompanies imposter syndrome.

Emotional Support:

Peers can offer empathy and understanding, which can be incredibly comforting during difficult times. Emotional support from peers can come in many forms, such as listening without judgment, offering words of encouragement, or simply being present. This type of support is crucial because it helps service members feel seen and understood. For example, if someone is struggling with feelings of inadequacy after a failed mission, their peers can provide reassurance and remind them of their past successes and strengths. This emotional backing can help counteract the negative self-talk that fuels imposter syndrome and boost overall morale.

Practical Advice:

Peers can share strategies and coping mechanisms that have worked for them, providing practical tools to manage stress and self-doubt. This advice is often practical and grounded in real-world experience, making it immediately applicable. For instance, a peer might suggest specific relaxation techniques, such as deep breathing exercises, to use before a stressful evaluation or share tips on maintaining a healthy work-life balance to prevent burnout. These shared strategies can be incredibly valuable, as they come from individuals who understand the specific context and demands of military life. By adopting these practical tools, military members can develop better coping mechanisms to handle the pressures they face and reduce the impact of imposter syndrome.

Mentors:

Mentors provide guidance, wisdom, and perspective that come from experience. Having a mentor who has navigated similar challenges can be immensely reassuring. They can offer a broader perspective on personal and professional growth, helping mentees see beyond their current struggles.

How Mentors Help:

Guidance and Advice:

Mentors can provide valuable advice on career progression and personal development, helping mentees navigate complex situations. With their extensive experience and knowledge, mentors can offer insights that mentees might not have considered. For example, a mentor can help a service member identify their strengths and areas for improvement, create a strategic plan for career advancement, and provide tips on effective leadership. This guidance can be particularly helpful when facing pivotal career decisions, such as choosing specialized training or considering a transition to a new role. Mentors can also offer advice on balancing professional responsibilities with personal life, which is crucial for maintaining overall well-being.

Perspective:

Mentors can offer a broader view of success and failure, helping to alleviate the pressure of perfectionism. They can share their own experiences of setbacks and achievements, demonstrating that failure is a natural part of growth and success is often a result of perseverance through challenges. For instance, a mentor might recount a time when they faced a significant obstacle, how they overcame it, and what they learned from the experience. This perspective can help mentees see their own struggles in a different light, reducing the fear of failure and encouraging a more resilient mindset. Understanding that even the most successful individuals have faced and overcome difficulties can be incredibly reassuring.

Role Modeling:

Seeing how mentors have overcome their own obstacles can inspire and motivate mentees to persist through their challenges. Mentors serve as living examples of resilience, determination, and success. By observing their mentors' journeys, mentees can learn valuable lessons about perseverance, adaptability, and the importance of maintaining a positive attitude. For example, if a mentor shares how they dealt with imposter syndrome early in their career and the strategies they used to build confidence, it can provide a roadmap for mentees facing similar issues. This role modeling not only offers practical strategies but also instills hope and motivation, showing that it is possible to overcome difficulties and achieve one's goals.

Mental Health Professionals:

Mental health professionals bring a wealth of expertise in addressing psychological issues. They can help service members develop effective strategies to combat imposter syndrome, such as cognitive-behavioral techniques and mindfulness practices.

How Mental Health Professionals Help:

Expertise:

Therapists and counselors have specialized training to address mental health issues, providing evidence-based techniques to manage anxiety and self-doubt. They are equipped with a deep understanding of psychological theories and practical skills to help individuals cope with various mental health challenges. For instance, Cognitive Behavioral Therapy (CBT) is a common approach used to change negative thought patterns and behaviors associated with imposter syndrome. Therapists might also employ techniques such as mindfulness-based stress reduction (MBSR) to help individuals stay present and manage stress more effectively. This expertise ensures that military members receive high-quality care tailored to their specific mental health needs, helping them build resilience and improve their overall well-being.

Confidentiality:

Sessions with mental health professionals are confidential, allowing service members to discuss their issues openly without fear of judgment. This safe and private environment encourages individuals to share their deepest concerns and insecurities, which they might be reluctant to discuss with peers or superiors. Knowing that their conversations are protected by confidentiality fosters a sense of trust and security, making it easier for service members to be honest and open about their struggles. This openness is crucial for effective therapy, as it allows the therapist to gain a comprehensive understanding of the individual's challenges and develop a more accurate and effective treatment plan.

Personalized Support:

Mental health professionals can tailor their approaches to the individual's specific needs, ensuring that the support provided is highly effective. Each person's experience with imposter syndrome is unique, and a one-size-fits-all approach is rarely effective. Therapists conduct thorough assessments to understand the individual's history, personality, and specific challenges. Based on this information, they create personalized treatment plans that might include a combination of therapeutic techniques, such as CBT, mindfulness practices, and psychoeducation. This customized approach ensures that the therapy addresses the root causes of the individual's issues and provides them with practical tools to manage their symptoms. Additionally, therapists can adjust their methods as the individual progresses, ensuring that the support remains relevant and effective throughout the therapeutic journey.

Benefits of Community in Overcoming Imposter Syndrome:

Shared Understanding:

One of the primary benefits of being part of a community or a tight-knit group is the shared understanding of experiences. In a military context, service members often face similar challenges, pressures, and expectations. Being surrounded by individuals who have gone through or are going through the same experiences can be incredibly validating. This shared understanding helps to normalize feelings of self-doubt and inadequacy, making it easier for individuals to accept that imposter syndrome is a common experience rather than a personal failing. For example, sharing stories about common struggles during group discussions can help individuals see that they are not alone, which can significantly reduce feelings of isolation and self-doubt.

Emotional Support:

Community and camaraderie provide a robust emotional support network. The bonds formed within a supportive group create an environment where individuals feel safe to express their fears and insecurities. This emotional support can come in various forms, such as offering a listening ear, providing words of encouragement, or simply being present during tough times. For instance, during a challenging deployment or a stressful training period, having a group of peers who offer encouragement and support can make a significant difference in managing stress and maintaining mental health. This emotional backing helps build resilience and provides a buffer against the negative impact of imposter syndrome.

Encouragement and Motivation:

Being part of a community where members encourage each other promotes a positive atmosphere of growth and development. When individuals see their peers achieving goals and overcoming obstacles, it can serve as a powerful motivator. Positive reinforcement from peers can boost self-esteem and confidence. For example, when a military member receives praise or recognition from their unit for their contributions, it can reinforce their sense of competence and worth. This collective encouragement helps individuals to focus on their strengths and accomplishments rather than their perceived shortcomings.

Opportunities for Peer Learning:

Communities provide opportunities for learning and personal growth through peer interactions. By sharing knowledge, skills, and experiences, members can learn from each other and develop new strategies to cope with challenges. For instance, more experienced service members can mentor newer recruits, offering advice on navigating the military environment and managing imposter syndrome. These learning opportunities can help individuals develop better coping mechanisms and build their confidence in their abilities.

Building Trust and Confidence:

Camaraderie fosters a sense of trust and belonging, which is essential for building confidence. When individuals feel that they are a valued part of a community, their sense of self-worth is reinforced. Trusting relationships within a group allow individuals to take risks, try new things, and grow without the fear of harsh judgment or failure. For example, participating in team-building exercises or collaborative missions helps build trust among team members, enhancing overall confidence and reducing the impact of imposter syndrome.

In the battle against imposter syndrome, the power of connection cannot be overstated. Seeking support from peers, mentors, and mental health professionals plays a crucial role in overcoming feelings of inadequacy and self-doubt. Through shared experiences and emotional backing, peers provide a unique perspective and practical advice that is both relatable and comforting. Mentors, with their wisdom and experience, offer guidance and role modeling that help individuals navigate their challenges and see the bigger picture. Mental health professionals bring specialized expertise and confidentiality, offering personalized strategies to manage and mitigate imposter syndrome.

Equally important is the sense of community that military life fosters. The bonds formed within units and groups provide a safe space for service members to express their vulnerabilities and receive encouragement. This collective support system not only normalizes the struggles associated with imposter syndrome but also builds resilience and confidence through shared understanding, emotional support, and peer learning.

Finally, embracing these connections and seeking support within a community can transform the isolating experience of imposter syndrome into an opportunity for growth and self-acceptance. By creating authentic relationships and tapping into the collective strength of their community, military members can overcome the inner critic and find a renewed sense of purpose and belonging.

CHAPTER 9

EMBRACING YOUR VALOR
CULTIVATING CONFIDENCE AND AUTHENTICITY

In the demanding and often harsh world of the military, service members are conditioned to prioritize mission success and team cohesion over individual recognition. While this focus on collective achievement is crucial, it can sometimes lead to neglecting personal strengths, accomplishments, and unique qualities. The weight of high expectations, relentless comparisons, and the pressure to maintain a façade of invulnerability often overshadow the importance of embracing one's own valor.

This chapter, "Embracing Your Valor: Cultivating Confidence and Authenticity," aims to shift that narrative. It encourages readers to take a step back and recognize their own worth, celebrating their strengths and achievements rather than diminishing them. Embracing your valor means acknowledging the qualities that make you unique and valuable, not just to your unit, but to yourself.

Throughout this chapter, we will explore practical, actionable steps to help cultivate confidence and authenticity. Confidence isn't about never feeling fear or doubt; it's about acknowledging those feelings and moving forward with purpose. Authenticity means being true to who you are, embracing your strengths and vulnerabilities alike. By integrating these principles into daily life, service members can build a stronger, more resilient self-identity that withstands the pressures of both military and civilian environments.

You can expect to delve into strategies that encourage self-recognition and appreciation, such as setting realistic personal goals, engaging in positive self-talk, and seeking feedback from trusted peers and mentors. We will discuss ways to build and maintain a confident demeanor, even in the face of setbacks, and the importance of being genuine in your interactions with others.

This journey towards confidence and authenticity is not about becoming someone else; it's about becoming more of who you already are. By the end of this chapter, you will have a toolkit of techniques to help you recognize your own valor and cultivate a mindset that honors your true self, empowering you to face challenges with a fortified sense of self-worth and integrity.

Embrace Your Strengths, Accomplishments, and Unique Qualities

Recognizing and Valuing Your Strengths:

One of the first steps in embracing your strengths is to take a moment to acknowledge them. In the military, there is often a strong emphasis on teamwork and collective achievement, which can sometimes lead individuals to downplay their own contributions. However, recognizing your personal strengths is crucial for building confidence and self-esteem.

Start by identifying the skills and abilities that set you apart. These could be technical skills, such as proficiency with certain equipment or procedures, or soft skills, like effective communication, leadership, or problem-solving abilities. Reflect on feedback you've received from peers and superiors – what do they frequently commend you for? What tasks or responsibilities do you handle with ease that others might find challenging?

Celebrating Your Accomplishments:

It's essential to celebrate your achievements, both big and small. Military culture often emphasizes continuous improvement and striving for the next goal, which can sometimes overshadow past successes. However, taking time to recognize and celebrate your accomplishments helps reinforce your capabilities and strengths.

Keep a record of your achievements. This could be a journal, a digital document, or a collection of certificates and commendations. Regularly review this record to remind yourself of your successes and the progress you've made over time. Celebrating accomplishments doesn't mean resting on your laurels, but rather using past successes as a foundation for future growth.

Embracing Your Unique Qualities:

Everyone has unique qualities that contribute to their identity and value within a team. These qualities might include your cultural background, personal experiences, perspectives, and even quirks. Embracing these unique aspects of yourself is vital for authenticity and confidence.

Reflect on what makes you unique. Consider how your background and experiences have shaped your approach to challenges and your interactions with others. Recognize that these unique qualities are strengths, not liabilities. They add to the diversity and richness of the team and bring different viewpoints and solutions to the table.

Positive Self-Talk and Affirmations:

Changing the way you talk to yourself can have a significant impact on how you perceive your strengths and accomplishments. Practice positive self-talk by replacing self-critical thoughts with affirmations that reinforce your value and abilities. For example, instead of thinking, "I'm not good enough," tell yourself, "I am capable and have proven my skills through my achievements."

Create a list of affirmations that resonate with you. Read them daily, especially during times of doubt or stress. Over time, these positive messages can help shift your mindset towards greater self-acceptance and confidence.

Seeking and Acting on Feedback:

Constructive feedback from trusted peers and mentors is invaluable for recognizing and embracing your strengths. Seek out feedback regularly and view it as an opportunity for growth rather than criticism. When you receive positive feedback, take it to heart and allow it to bolster your confidence. When feedback highlights areas for improvement, use it as a roadmap for further development.

Building a Support Network:

Surround yourself with individuals who support and uplift you. Whether it's friends, family, peers, or mentors, having a support network can reinforce your self-worth and provide encouragement. Engage with people who recognize and celebrate your strengths and accomplishments, and who remind you of your unique value when you doubt yourself.

Engaging in Self-Reflection:

Regular self-reflection can help you stay connected with your strengths and accomplishments. Set aside time each week to reflect on what you've achieved, the challenges you've overcome, and the qualities you've demonstrated. Use this reflection to plan for future goals and to reinforce your belief in your abilities.

Actionable Steps for Cultivating Confidence and Authenticity

1. Set Realistic Goals:

Setting achievable goals is a crucial step in building confidence. When you set goals that are challenging yet attainable, you give yourself clear targets to strive for and celebrate upon completion.

How to Practice:

Break Down Goals: Divide larger goals into smaller, manageable tasks. This makes the goal less overwhelming and allows you to track progress more easily.

Set SMART Goals: Ensure your goals are Specific, Measurable, Achievable, Relevant, and Time-bound.

Celebrate Milestones: Acknowledge and celebrate each milestone you reach on the way to your larger goals. This reinforces your progress and boosts confidence.

2. Engage in Positive Self-Talk:

The way you talk to yourself has a significant impact on your self-confidence. Replacing negative thoughts with positive affirmations can help cultivate a more supportive internal dialogue.

How to Practice:

Identify Negative Thoughts: Pay attention to moments when you are self-critical. Note the specific thoughts that undermine your confidence.

Reframe Thoughts: Replace negative thoughts with positive affirmations. For example, instead of thinking, "I can't do this," tell yourself, "I am capable and prepared."

Daily Affirmations: Start each day by repeating positive affirmations that reinforce your strengths and abilities. Over time, this practice can reshape your mindset.

3. Practice Self-Compassion:

Being kind to yourself is essential for both confidence and authenticity. Self-compassion involves treating yourself with the same kindness and understanding that you would offer to a friend.

How to Practice:

Supportive Self-Talk: When you make a mistake, avoid harsh self-criticism. Instead, speak to yourself with kindness and encouragement.

Write Compassionate Letters: Write letters to yourself from the perspective of a supportive friend. Highlight your strengths and offer comforting words for your struggles.

Engage in Acts of Kindness: Treat yourself to small acts of kindness, such as taking time to relax, enjoying a favorite hobby, or simply giving yourself a break.

4. Seek Feedback and Learn from It:

Constructive feedback from trusted individuals can provide valuable insights and reinforce your confidence. Learning to view feedback as a tool for growth rather than criticism is key.

How to Practice:

Ask for Feedback: Regularly seek feedback from peers, mentors, and supervisors. Be specific about the areas where you would like input.

Reflect on Feedback: Take time to reflect on the feedback you receive. Identify actionable steps you can take to improve and grow.

Implement Changes: Use the feedback to make positive changes. Acknowledging and acting on feedback shows a commitment to personal and professional growth.

5. Embrace Vulnerability:

Authenticity involves being open about your strengths and weaknesses. Embracing vulnerability can help you connect with others and build deeper, more genuine relationships.

How to Practice:

Share Your Experiences: Open up to trusted peers and mentors about your challenges and successes. Sharing your experiences can foster a sense of connection and support.

Be Honest with Yourself: Acknowledge your fears and insecurities. Accepting these parts of yourself is the first step towards authentic self-expression.

Practice Transparency: In both professional and personal settings, strive to be honest and transparent. This builds trust and authenticity in your relationships.

6. Develop a Support Network:

Surrounding yourself with supportive individuals can significantly enhance your confidence and authenticity. A strong support network provides encouragement and helps you stay grounded.

How to Practice:

Identify Supportive People: Identify friends, family members, peers, and mentors who offer positive support and encouragement.

Engage Regularly: Maintain regular contact with your support network. Share your experiences, seek advice, and offer support in return.

Join Communities: Participate in groups or communities where members share similar interests and goals. This can provide additional support and a sense of belonging.

7. Reflect on Your Values and Strengths:

Taking time to reflect on your core values and strengths can help reinforce your sense of self-worth and authenticity. Understanding what truly matters to you guides your actions and decisions.

How to Practice:

Identify Core Values: Reflect on the values that are most important to you. Write them down and consider how they influence your actions and decisions.

Strengths Inventory: Make a list of your strengths and achievements. Review this list regularly to remind yourself of your capabilities.

Align Actions with Values: Ensure that your actions and decisions are aligned with your core values. This alignment fosters authenticity and confidence.

8. Engage in Activities that Build Confidence:

Participating in activities that challenge you and allow you to succeed can boost your confidence and help you grow.

How to Practice:

Take on New Challenges: Seek out opportunities that push you out of your comfort zone. Each new challenge is an opportunity to grow and build confidence.

Pursue Passions: Engage in activities that you are passionate about. Success in areas you love can enhance your overall sense of self-worth.

Reflect on Successes: After completing challenging activities, take time to reflect on what you learned and achieved. Use these reflections to build confidence for future endeavors.

Building confidence and embracing authenticity is a continuous journey, filled with moments of reflection and growth. By focusing on your strengths, recognizing your achievements, and appreciating your unique qualities, you can start to quiet the voice of self-doubt. Simple actions like setting achievable goals, practicing self-kindness, seeking constructive feedback, and allowing yourself to be vulnerable can create a solid base of self-assurance and genuine self-expression.

Confidence doesn't mean never making mistakes or always being perfect. It means understanding your worth and tackling challenges with a positive and resilient attitude. Authenticity involves being true to yourself and letting others see the real you, including your strengths and imperfections.

As you incorporate these practices into your daily routine, you'll likely notice a stronger and more secure sense of self. You'll realize that your worth isn't tied to your successes or failures but lies in who you are as a person. Whether in the military or any other aspect of life, embracing your valor and authenticity will help you overcome imposter syndrome and lead a more fulfilling and empowered life.

CHAPTER 10

FROM SHADOWS TO LIGHT

NAVIGATING IMPOSTER SYNDROME WITH COURAGE

Imposter syndrome can feel like a relentless shadow, constantly casting doubt on your achievements and abilities. In this final chapter, we'll shift our focus from the shadows to the light. It's about reflecting on your journey of self-discovery and growth, and learning how to face imposter syndrome with courage, resilience, and self-compassion.

Navigating imposter syndrome isn't about magically erasing self-doubt. It's about recognizing these feelings as part of your journey and finding ways to manage them. Throughout this book, we've explored various aspects of military life where imposter syndrome can take root – from the pressure of high expectations and role transitions to comparing yourself with peers and hiding vulnerabilities.

Now, it's time to bring all these insights together. We'll reflect on the personal growth you've experienced and the strengths you've discovered along the way. You'll learn practical strategies to confront imposter syndrome, transforming it from a source of anxiety into an opportunity for growth. This involves building resilience – the ability to bounce back from setbacks and keep moving forward – and practicing self-compassion, treating yourself with the same kindness and understanding you'd offer a close friend.

By adopting these qualities, you can start to see imposter syndrome not as an insurmountable obstacle but as a challenge you can manage with the right tools and mindset. This chapter aims to equip you with those tools, encouraging you to step out of the shadows and into the light of self-assurance and authenticity. Your journey is unique, and by navigating it with courage and resilience, you can turn self-doubt into a powerful force for personal and professional growth.

Reflecting on the Journey of Self-Discovery and Growth

Reflecting on your journey of self-discovery and growth is an essential part of overcoming imposter syndrome. This reflection allows you to appreciate how far you've come, recognize your achievements, and understand the lessons you've learned along the way. It's about seeing the bigger picture of your personal and professional development and acknowledging the steps you've taken to become who you are today.

Understanding Your Starting Point

Every journey begins with a starting point. For many in the military, this may have been the day you first enlisted, full of uncertainty and perhaps a bit of fear about what lay ahead. Reflecting on this starting point helps you see the immense progress you've made. Consider the skills you've developed, the knowledge you've acquired, and the experiences that have shaped you. This isn't just about the technical skills of your military role but also about the personal growth that has occurred – the resilience, discipline, and leadership abilities that have become part of your character.

Recognizing Achievements and Milestones

In the hustle of daily life, especially in the demanding environment of the military, it's easy to overlook your achievements. Take a moment to list the milestones you've reached. These can be big accomplishments, like completing a challenging training program or receiving a promotion, as well as smaller victories, like successfully navigating a difficult conversation or learning a new skill. Each of these milestones shows your hard work, dedication, and capability. Recognizing them helps to build a narrative of success that counters the negative voice of the inner critic.

Learning from Challenges and Setbacks

No journey is without its challenges and setbacks. Reflecting on these moments is crucial because they often provide the most significant opportunities for growth. Think about a time when you faced a particularly tough challenge. How did you respond? What did you learn from the experience? How did it change you? By analyzing these moments, you can identify patterns of resilience and problem-solving that you might not have noticed in the moment. These reflections highlight your ability to overcome adversity and adapt, reinforcing your self-worth and capability.

Embracing Change and Transformation

Self-discovery often involves adopting change and transformation. This could mean adapting to new roles, shifting your mindset, or developing new habits. Reflect on the transformations you've undergone – how you've changed as a person, how your perspectives have shifted, and how your values have evolved. This process of transformation is a powerful indicator of growth. It shows that you are not static but a dynamic individual capable of continuous improvement.

Connecting Past and Present

Finally, reflection allows you to connect your past experiences with your present self. It helps you see how your history has shaped your current abilities and attitudes. This connection is vital for understanding your journey comprehensively. By seeing the continuum of your growth, you can better appreciate your current strengths and prepare for future challenges with confidence.

How to Navigate Imposter Syndrome

Navigating imposter syndrome with courage, resilience, and self-compassion is a powerful approach that empowers you to face self-doubt head-on and transform it into a source of personal growth. Here's how you can cultivate these qualities to overcome imposter syndrome:

Courage

Courage isn't the absence of fear but the determination to act despite it. Facing imposter syndrome requires the bravery to acknowledge your feelings of inadequacy and challenge them. Here are some steps to help you build courage:

Acknowledge Your Feelings: Admit to yourself that you're experiencing imposter syndrome. Recognize that these feelings are common and don't define your worth or abilities.

Speak Up: Share your experiences with trusted friends, family, or colleagues. Talking about your fears can diminish their power and help you realize that you're not alone.

Take Risks: Step out of your comfort zone and embrace new challenges. Each time you face your fears, you build your confidence and prove to yourself that you are capable.

Resilience

Resilience is the ability to bounce back from setbacks and keep moving forward. It's about staying strong in the face of hardship and using difficulties as opportunities for growth. Here's how to develop resilience:

Reframe Setbacks: Instead of seeing setbacks as failures, view them as learning experiences. Ask yourself what you can learn from each challenge and how it can make you stronger.

Build a Support System: Surround yourself with supportive people who can offer encouragement and advice. Lean on them during tough times and offer support in return.

Practice Self-Care: Take care of your physical and mental well-being. Exercise regularly, eat healthily, get enough sleep, and engage in activities that bring you joy and relaxation.

Self-Compassion

Self-compassion involves treating yourself with the same kindness and understanding you would offer to a friend. It's about being gentle with yourself when you make mistakes and recognizing your inherent worth. Here's how to cultivate self-compassion:

Supportive Self-Talk: Replace self-critical thoughts with compassionate ones. When you catch yourself being harsh, pause and reframe your thoughts as you would for a friend.

Mindful Awareness: Practice mindfulness to become aware of your thoughts and feelings without judgment. Acknowledge your emotions and allow yourself to experience them without trying to suppress or change them.

Celebrate Your Achievements: Take time to acknowledge and celebrate your accomplishments, no matter how small. Recognize your efforts and give yourself credit for your successes.

In concluding this chapter, it's essential to recognize the transformative power that lies within each of us to navigate imposter syndrome with courage, resilience, and self-compassion. The journey through self-doubt is not an easy one, but it is a path that can lead to personal growth and a deeper understanding of our true worth.

Reflecting on the Journey

As you reflect on the experiences and insights shared in this chapter, remember that the feelings of inadequacy and self-doubt are not indicators of your actual abilities or worth. They are simply part of the human experience, especially in high-pressure environments like the military. Acknowledge your struggles, but also celebrate your strengths and accomplishments.

Embracing Courage

It takes immense courage to confront imposter syndrome. By facing your fears and speaking openly about your experiences, you break the cycle of isolation and self-criticism. Each act of bravery, no matter how small, reinforces your resilience and demonstrates your capacity to thrive in the face of adversity.

Building Resilience

Resilience is built through overcoming challenges and learning from setbacks. Every time you pick yourself up after a fall, you strengthen your ability to cope with future obstacles. By reframing setbacks as opportunities for growth, you transform them into stepping stones toward greater confidence and self-assurance.

Practicing Self-Compassion

Self-compassion is the foundation of lasting change. Treat yourself with the kindness and understanding you deserve. Recognize that everyone has moments of doubt and that making mistakes is part of the learning process. By being gentle with yourself, you create a supportive inner environment where you can flourish.

Navigating imposter syndrome requires ongoing effort and dedication. It's a continuous journey of self-discovery and personal growth. Embrace your unique qualities and recognize that your value extends far beyond your achievements. By adopting courage, resilience, and self-compassion, you can overcome imposter syndrome and step confidently into your true potential.

Remember, you are not alone. There is a community of peers, mentors, and professionals ready to support you. Lean on them, share your journey, and offer your support in return. Together, you can move from the shadows of self-doubt into the light of self-assurance and authentic self-worth.

Wipe the slate clean. And rewrite it. No fairy tales. Be your own narrator. And go for a happy ending. One foot in front of the other. You will make it.

- Shonda Rimes

ABOUT THE AUTHOR

Dr. Joshan Flowers, a retired Air Force Master Sergeant, brings a wealth of experience and expertise to the table. With a distinguished military career and a passion for leadership and personal development, Dr. Flowers has become a recognized authority in the fields of strategic leadership and Imposter Syndrome.

In addition to her professional accomplishments, Dr. Flowers is the author of the insightful book, Imposter Syndrome: Silencing the Self-Doubt Within the Workplace. Drawing from her extensive experience, Dr. Flowers offers practical solutions for individuals seeking to overcome self-doubt and excel in their careers.

Made in the USA
Middletown, DE
17 January 2026